INTRODUCING

Sanguine

40 Powerful Devotionals

BY

JENNIFER HILL

SUMMERLAND PUBLISHING

ISBN: 978-0-9963736-5-4

Copyright 2016 by Jennifer Hill

All rights reserved. Except for use in any review, the reproduction or utilization of this work in whole or in part in any form by any electronic, mechanical or other means, now known or hereafter invented, including xerography, photocopying and recording, or in any information storage or retrieval system, is forbidden without the written permission of the publisher, Summerland Publishing, 887 Hanson Street, Bozeman, MT 59718 www.summerlandpublishing.com

Printed in the United States of America.

Library of Congress Control Number: 2016939952

To my beautiful babies

Tyler Jordan Ried
Destiny Jada Copeland
Amber Marie Ruby Ried
Grandbaby #2

you just call out my name,
and you know wherever I am,
I'll come running…**

LGB
LOVE GOD BLESS
THE MOMMY
A.K.A
PATTY CAKES

**"You've Got a Friend" by James Taylor

Introduction

The Bible uses the number 40 to denote completion or fulfillment. It is the number for the duration of a trial of any kind. The meaning of Sanguine (pronounced sanG gwen) is to be optimistic or positive, especiallly in an apparently bad or difficult situation. I encourage you to study these divine devotionals for 40 days, and I assure you the outcome will be fascinating!

40 Powerful Devotionals

Sanguine

1

If you're alive, there is a purpose for your life...

※※※

Ecclesiastes 3:1

To everything there is a season, and a time to every purpose under the Heaven

2

Be so happy
that it becomes
contagious!

Psalm 31:7

I will be glad and rejoice in the mercy; for thou hast considered my trouble; thou hast known my soul in adversities.

3

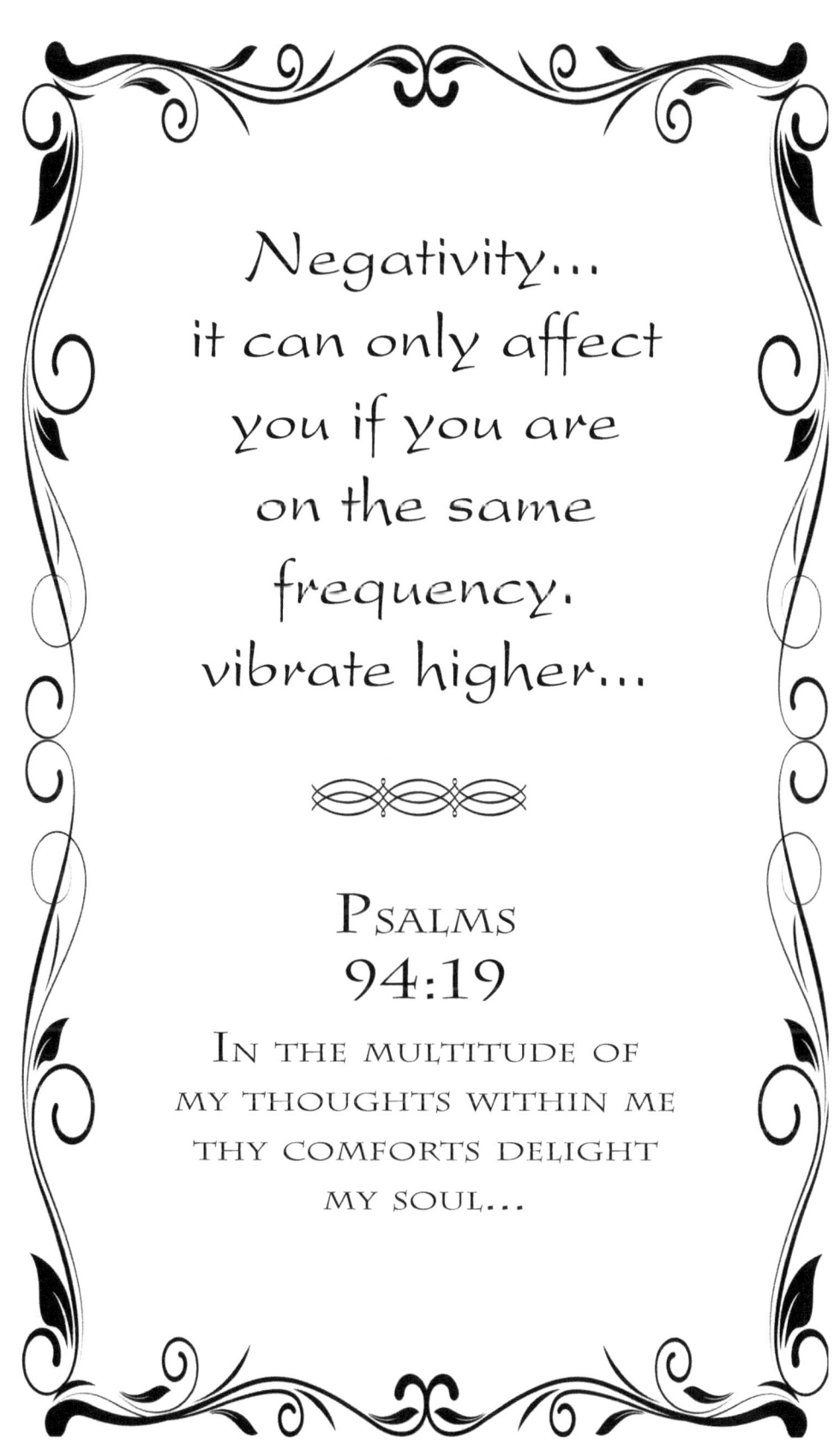

Negativity...
it can only affect
you if you are
on the same
frequency.
vibrate higher...

Psalms 94:19

In the multitude of my thoughts within me thy comforts delight my soul...

4

Don't forget whose you are...

1 John 4:4

YE ARE OF GOD, LITTLE CHILDREN AND HAVE OVERCOME THEM: BECAUSE GREATER IS HE THAT IS IN YOU, THAN HE THAT IS IN THE WORLD…

5

Don't be blinded by the lies of the world. Be enlightened by the truth of God's love.

Romans 12:2

And be not conformed to this world: but be ye transformed by the renewing of your mind, that ye may prove what is that good, and acceptable, and perfect will of God

6

The next time you feel like giving up…

<u>Try Again</u>

Joshua 1:9

Have not I commanded thee? Be strong and of a good courage; be not afraid, neither be thou dismayed: For the Lord thy God is with thee whither so ever thou goest.

7

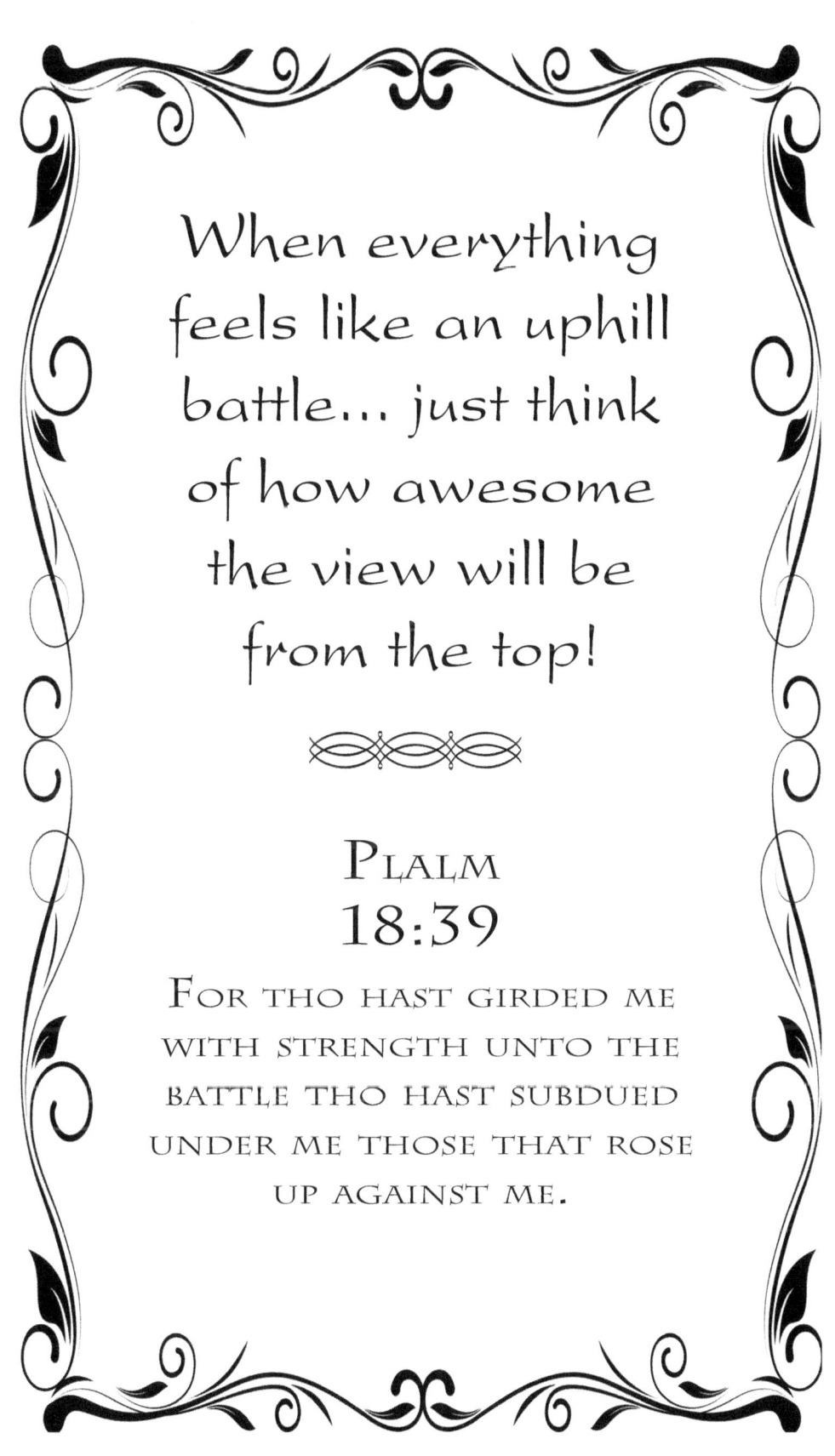

When everything feels like an uphill battle... just think of how awesome the view will be from the top!

PLALM 18:39

FOR THO HAST GIRDED ME WITH STRENGTH UNTO THE BATTLE THO HAST SUBDUED UNDER ME THOSE THAT ROSE UP AGAINST ME.

8

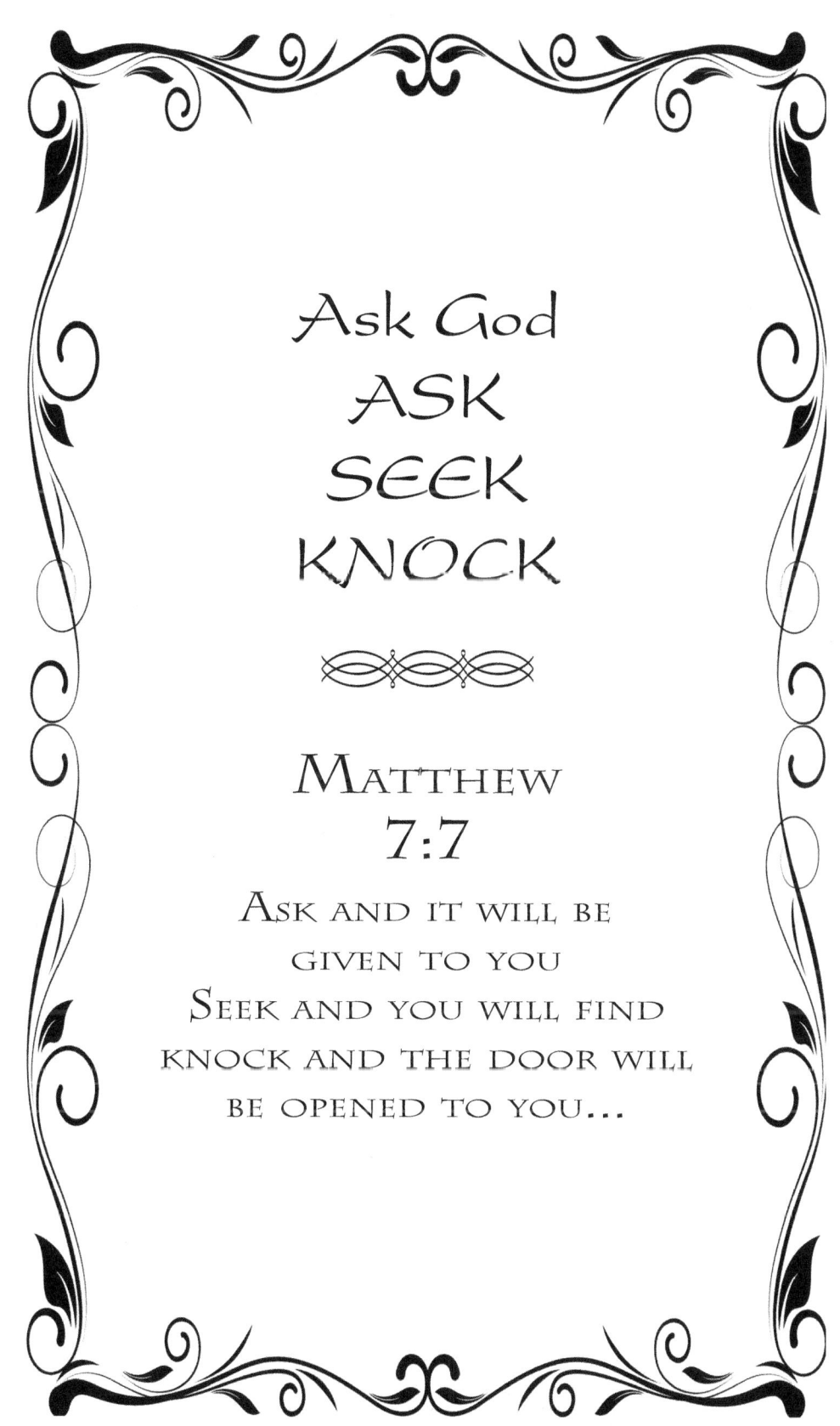

9

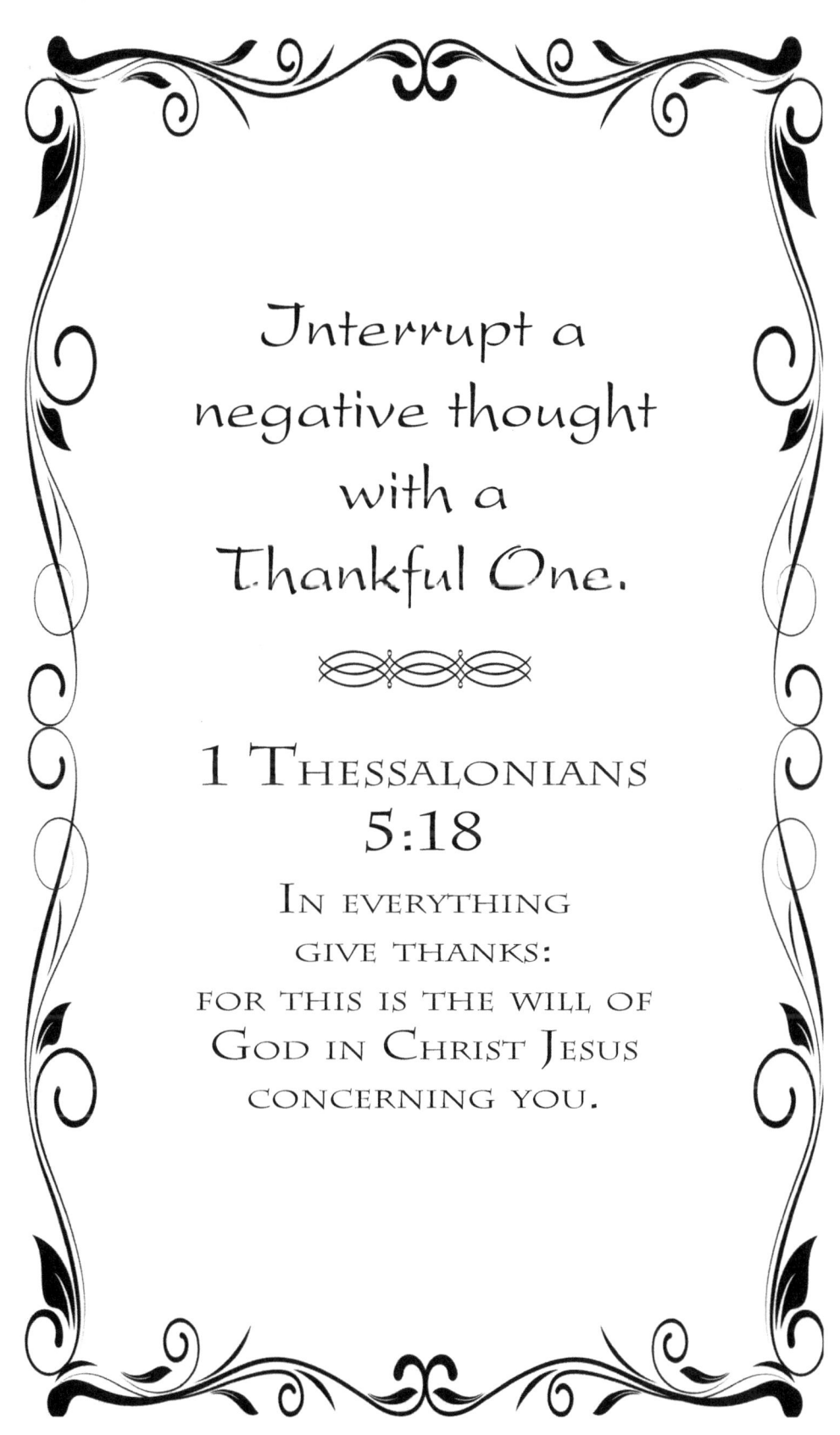

Interrupt a negative thought with a Thankful One.

1 Thessalonians 5:18

In everything give thanks: for this is the will of God in Christ Jesus concerning you.

10

Prioritize

Matthew 6:33

But seek ye first the kingdom of God, and his righteousness; and all these things shall be added unto you.

11

Every moment is a profound opportunity to do good.

Gelatians 6:10

As we have therefore opportunity, let us do good unto all men, especially unto them who are of the household of faith.

12

Praise God even when you don't understand what He is doing…

Proverbs 3:5

Trust in the Lord with all thine heart; and lean not unto thine own understanding.

13

Enter into each day with greatness!

Great + Attitude

=

Gratitude

---

1 Chronicles 29:11

Thine, O Lord, is the greatness, and the power and the glory, and the victory, and the majesty; for all that is in the Heaven and in the earth is thine; thine is the kingdom, O Lord; and thou art exalted as head above all...

14

Be fearless and valiant!

※※※

Psalm 118:6

The Lord is on my side; I will not fear: what can man do unto me?

15

Don't dwell
in confusion…

Corinthians 14:33

For God is not the author of confusion, but of peace, as in all churches of the saints…

16

17

Begin each day rejoicing!

Psalm 118:24

This is the day which the Lord hath made; we will rejoice and be glad in it!

18

Stay strong and hold on...God's plans for you are so incredible your mind can't even fathom them!

Jeremiah 29:11

For I know the thoughts that I think toward you, saith the Lord. thoughts of peace and not of evil, to give you an expected end.

19

Self confidence is the very best outfit you can ever wear...

Ephesians 6:11

Put on the whole armor of God, that ye may be able to stand against the wiles of the devil...

20

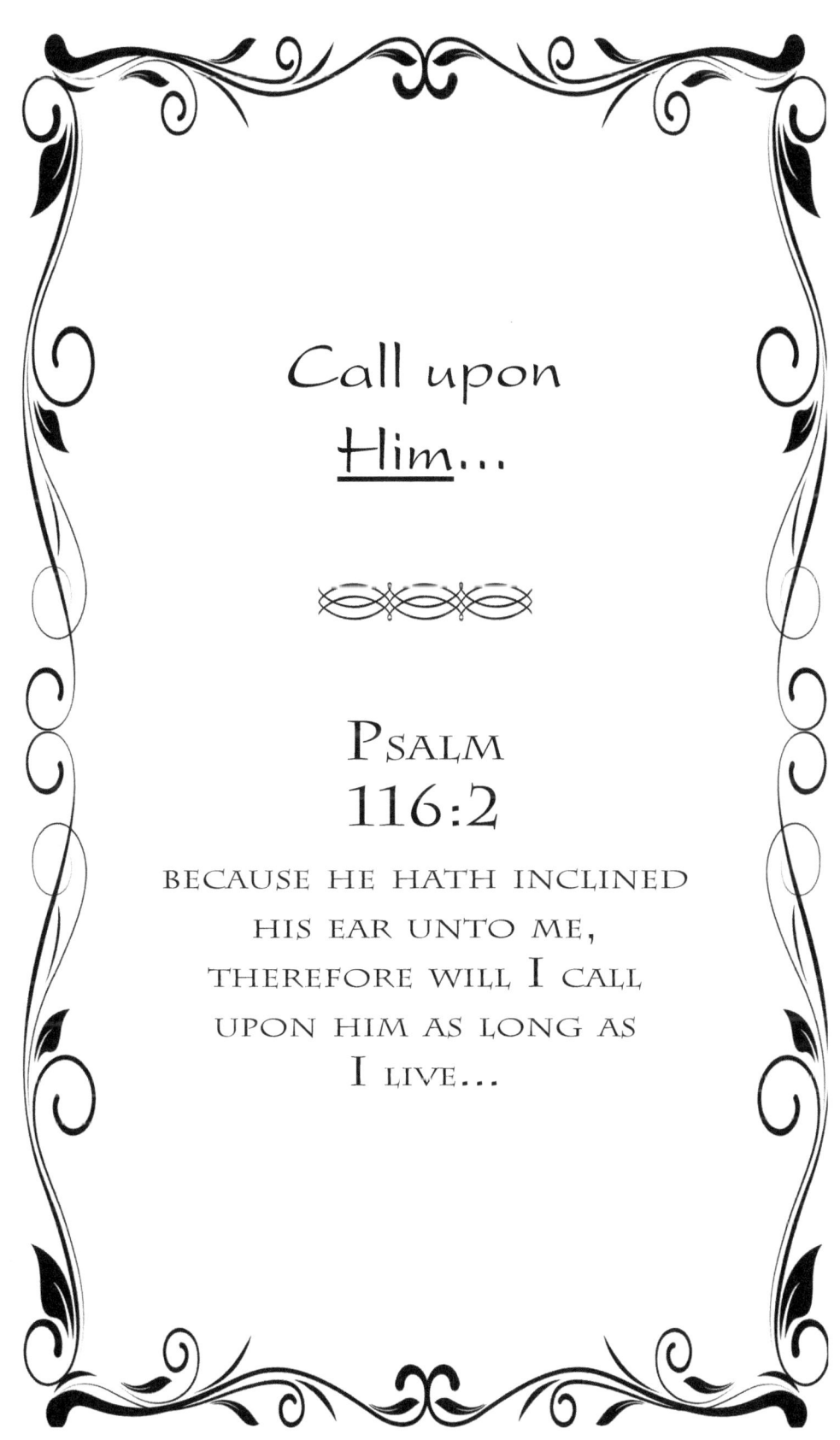

Call upon <u>Him</u>…

Psalm 116:2

Because he hath inclined his ear unto me, therefore will I call upon him as long as I live…

21

Practice Patience...

Isiah 40:31

But they that wait upon the Lord shall renew their strength; they shall mount up with wings as eagles; they shall run, and not be weary: and they shall walk, and not faint.

22

Be your Best You!

Exodus 32:29

For Moses had said, consecreate yourselves today to the Lord, even every man upon his son, and upon his brother; that he may bestow upon you a blessing this day

23

Breathe....
breathe in
His Grace
and exhale
with
Praise!

※※※

Ephesians
2:8
For buy GRACE ye
are saved through faith;
and that not of
yourselves:
it is the gift of
GOD!

24

See the glass half full—not half empty—then fill it the rest of the way up!

Ezra 10:4

Arise: for this matter belongeth unto thee: we also will be with thee: be of good courage and do it!

25

The Lord hears
your tears...

Psalm 35:17

The righteous cry, and the Lord heareth, and delivereth them out of all their troubles...

26

You have shelter from the storm...

Psalm 25:5

For in the time of trouble he shall hide me in his pavilion: in the secret of his tabernacle shall he hide me; he shall set me upon a rock...

27

It's a wonderful day to have a wonderful day!!!

Romans 12:12

Rejoicing in hope; patient in tribulation; continuing instant in prayer;

28

Stand on God's word...

Matthew 24:35

"Heaven and earth shall pass away, but my words shall not pass away"...

29

Focus on TODAY...

Matthew 6:34

Take therefore no thought for the morrow: for the morrow shall take thought for the things of itself. Sufficient unto the day is the evil thereof...

30

God is everywhere therefore pray anywhere...

Thessalonians 5:17
Pray without ceasing...

31

Be decisive...

Kings 18:21

And Elijah came unto all the people and said how long hath ye between two options? If the Lord be God, follow him: but if Baal, then follow him: and the people answered him not a word...

32

You are divinely protected…

PSALMS 121:7

THE LORD SHALL PRESERVE THEE FROM ALL EVIL: HE SHALL PRESERVE THY SOUL…

33

Remain strong…
you will be
Victorious…

1John 5:4

For whatsoever is born of God overcometh the world: and this is the victory that overcometh the world, even our faith…

34

Strive
for
Utopia...

※※※

Matthew 5:48

Be ye therefore perfect, even as your father which is in Heaven is perfect.

35

Positive thinking envokes positive energy!

Philippians 4:8

Finally brethen, whatsoever things are true: whatsoever things are honest: whatsoever things are just: whatsoever things are pure: whatsoever things are lovely: whatsoever things are of good report; if there be any virtue, and if there be any praise think on these things…

36

Start making GOD your reason to live, and YOU will never have a reason to quit.

Luke 20:38

For He is not a GOD of the dead, but of the living. For all live unto HIM.

37

Trust
GOD
and you will have
perfect peace…

Isiah
26:3-4

Thou wilt keep him in perfect peace whose mind is stayed on thee: because He trusteth in thee.

38

Answers are found in prayer.

Matthew 21:22

And all things whatsoever ye shall ask in prayer, believing, ye shall receive.

39

You are a walking, breathing wondrous work of GOD...

Job 33:4

The spirit of God hath made me, and the breath of the almigty hath given me life.

Ephesians 2:10

For we are his workmanship, created in Christ Jesus unto good works which God hath before ordained that we should walk in them.

40

Wait...

Psalm 27:14

Wait on the Lord: be of good courage, and he shall strengthen thine heart: WAIT I say, on the Lord.

Philippians 4:23

THE GRACE OF OUR LORD JESUS CHRIST BE WITH YOU ALL...

AMEN

The second definition of Sanguine is blood red. Beloved, the blood of Jesus cleanses us from all sin.

1 John 1:7-9

But if we walk in the light, as he is in the light, we have fellowship one with another, and the blood of Jesus Christ his son cleanseth us from all sin.

If you have not accepted Jesus Christ as your personal Lord and Savior, you can accept him now and your life will be changed forever.
I wish you everlasting peace and Love…

Jennifer L. Hill

A prayer that you may pray and ask Jesus to come into your heart and life.

Heavenly Father

I humbly come to you and sincerely repent of all my sins. I confess with my mouth that Jesus is Lord. I believe you raised him from the dead. I ask that Jesus will come into my life and be my Lord and Savior.
I now joyfully exclaim! Thank you Lord Jesus for saving me and cleansing me with your precious blood.
In Jesus name,

Amen....

Don't be blinded by the lies of the world. Be enlightened by the truth of God's love.

Romans 12:2

And be not conformed to this world: but be ye transformed by the renewing of your mind, that ye may prove what is that good, and acceptable, and perfect will of God.

www.ingramcontent.com/pod-product-compliance
Lightning Source LLC
Chambersburg PA
CBHW071733040426

42446CB00012B/2338